Birth and Death Certificates

England and Wales 18

Barbara Dix

Published 1999 Barbara Dixon
22 Redwood
Burnham
Berkshire SL1 8JN

ISBN 0 9535304 0 X

Design and production by Naomi Wright
Printed by Parchment (Oxford) Limited

Acknowledgements
I should like to thank all the following who helped or encouraged me: my colleague Leni Eves: Stan Worthington, Jenny Bartlett, and Mike Longworth for sending me certificates for publication; all those members of MLFHS and GenBrit on the Internet who sent comments and criticisms; my niece Naomi Wright for turning my first amateurish efforts into a professional finish; my mother Nora Bishop for proofreading (so any mistakes are hers now!); and lastly my husband John for his unfailing support and advice.

Contents

INTRODUCTION

This booklet has been prepared to try and help family historians first find and then make the most of the information provided by the birth and death certificates. It only relates to certificates issued by the registration service in England and Wales. (Scotland, Northern Ireland, Southern Ireland, the Isle of Man and the Channel Islands all have their own registration services which may differ significantly from the details discussed in this booklet.) In 1969 the format of the registers, and therefore the certificates issued from them changed considerably. This booklet is only relevant to the certificates issued from 1837 to 1969.

BIRTH CERTIFICATES

Birth Certificate Heading

This is one of the details on a birth certificate which is often ignored but it is of great relevance to family historians because it dictates which registration district name will appear in the indexes of the General Register Office, and the indexes, of course, are the starting point of your search. If you know how the registration districts were arrived at, then you might realise that you have been ignoring registrations that could be yours.

When civil registration was first organised the most obvious unit that already existed and could be adapted to registration districts was the Poor Law Unions. Many of the original districts were a straight use of these and indeed those who administered the Poor Laws often became the first Superintendent Registrars.

Poor Law Unions were made up of several parishes and the Unions could sometimes cross the county boundaries. As a registration district could be quite large – especially in rural areas – the actual place of birth could be quite a long way – and in a different county – from the town that gave its name to the registration district.

You will notice in the example shown of my grandmother's birth certificate (see page 2), that the registration district was Faringdon but the counties were Berkshire, Gloucestershire and Oxfordshire. Faringdon was then in Berkshire, but there would have been other places in Gloucestershire and Oxfordshire that came into the same registration district and would have had Faringdon in Berkshire as the registration district name. The moral of this is that if you can find a birth registration at the right time but apparently in the wrong place close by, it could be the one you have been looking for.

Some villages could lie in more than one registration district and in different counties e.g. the village of Colnbrook lay in three separate districts – one in Berkshire, one in Buckinghamshire and one in Surrey and this was not changed until 1994! So a family that moved down the road or across it could have children in totally different registration districts.

Registration districts also constantly changed as bits were taken from one registration district and given to another for administration reasons, so even

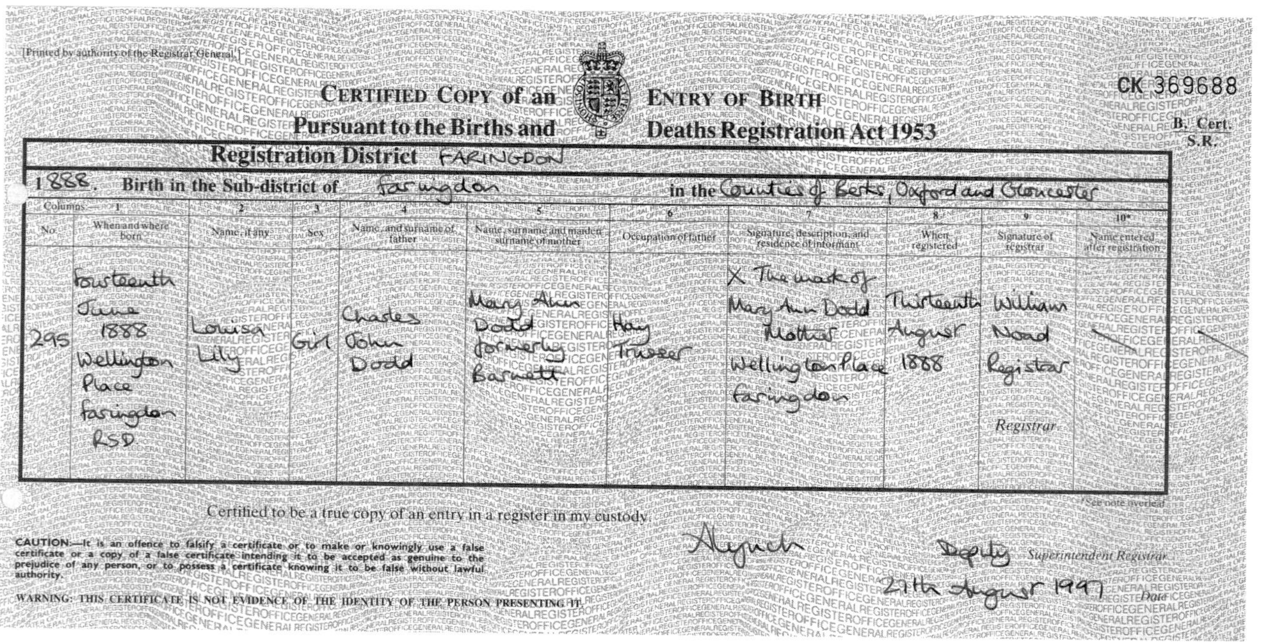

[Printed by authority of the Registrar General.]

CK 369688

B. Cert. S.R.

CERTIFIED COPY of an ENTRY OF BIRTH
Pursuant to the Births and Deaths Registration Act 1953

Registration District FARINGDON

1888. Birth in the Sub-district of Faringdon in the Counties of Berks, Oxford and Gloucester

Columns:—	1	2	3	4	5	6	7	8	9	10*
No.	When and where born	Name, if any	Sex	Name, and surname of father	Name, surname and maiden surname of mother	Occupation of father	Signature, description, and residence of informant	When registered	Signature of registrar	Name entered after registration
295	Fourteenth June 1888 Wellington Place Faringdon RSD	Louisa Lily	Girl	Charles John Dodd	Mary Ann Dodd formerly Barnett	Hay Trusser	X The mark of Mary Ann Dodd Mother Wellington Place Faringdon	Thirteenth August 1888	William Noad Registrar	—

Certified to be a true copy of an entry in a register in my custody.

A Lynch Deputy Superintendent Registrar

27th August 1997 Date

*See note overleaf

CAUTION.—It is an offence to falsify a certificate or to make or knowingly use a false certificate or a copy of a false certificate intending it to be accepted as genuine to the prejudice of any person, or to possess a certificate knowing it to be false without lawful authority.

WARNING: THIS CERTIFICATE IS NOT EVIDENCE OF THE IDENTITY OF THE PERSON PRESENTING IT.

Certificate of Louisa Lily Dodd

Apart from the heading with the 3 counties mentioned, this shows a registration where the informant (my great grandmother) couldn't read. Also it is a late registration, nearly 9 weeks after the baby was born. As a result, although my grandmother was born in June and might have been registered in the June quarter, her birth appears in the September quarter indexes. If the birth had been registered after more than 3 months, both the registrar and the superintendent registrar would have signed.

the same place might not have the same registration district name all through the years of registration. Even when the boundaries stayed much the same the registration district names were often changed e.g. we nearly missed a whole chunk of family because we did not realise that Great Boughton was the Chester district.

The secret is to be flexible – if you have the obvious registration where and when you expected it then that's fine but if you can't find the one you want then extract all the possible ones and start looking at the relationships between the place you want and the places that are given.

GRO reference

I think it is worth explaining how the GRO index references are built up. Once you know, you might find some short cuts to using them.

At the end of March, June, September and December, every registrar must send an accurate copy of every registration completed in the last quarter. These quarterly copies are then arranged in a set and specific sequence. First of all, England and Wales are divided into different areas and these give you the first element of the reference number and then each area is subdivided into smaller sub-areas and this gives you the second element of the reference Every sub-area has its registration districts arranged in the same order each time and the whole of one registration district's quarterly copies would be placed in order before moving on to the next registration district. Once the quarterly copies for a sub-area have been correctly arranged in order, they would be bound into a book (and these days microfilmed). If you have listed a lot of birth entries for a particular registration district you will probably have noticed how remarkably consistent the reference is – because the copies are assembled the same way every time.

So if you order a birth certificate for James Young March quarter 1859 Great Boughton 6a 197 it is a very precise reference. It tells the person producing your certificate for you to turn to the books (or microfilm) for 1859, find the March quarter book or film, look for area "6", then sub area "a" and turn to page 197. Page 197 will have 5 birth entries on it (before 1st April 1969) and the one required is for James Young. Bingo.

Now what else can you learn from the GRO reference? Well, you may be able to pick up the birth of twins because they are likely to have the identical reference:

e.g. SMALL Charles St Georges Ia 196
SMALL John St Georges Ia 196

might suggest that there were twins. However, the GRO reference is for a whole page of a register which means five entries. If you have twins on the same page they will have the same reference number. If, though, one twin was the last entry on one page and the other twin was the first on the next page they will have consecutive reference numbers not the same. And if two different families with the same surname are on the same page it will look like twins when it isn't. This is not as unusual as you might think – even with relatively uncommon names. Think of baptisms in Church registers and how often the same surname occurs on a page but the parents are different. I once saw three Thornton surnames in four entries and none of the families were related to one another.

It can sometimes be quicker to use the district and sub-district number rather than look for registration district names, or specific first names especially when doing a blanket search. As an example, my father's family name is Bishop which one might think was common enough. And so it is in the south, but in Yorkshire where the family comes from it is far less common. I find it much faster to run my finger down the numbers column and stop every time I see a "9" than to look for Skipton in the registration district name column.

Once you have found your reference and ordered your certificate, what does it tell you?

Entry Number

The first column on your birth certificate is the entry number in the register. Before 1st April 1969 this can be anything from 1 to 500.

Column 1 – Date And Place Of Birth

Date of birth

The date of birth should be clearly written in the form "Eighteenth May 1840" although some of the early registers have variations on that in the very first registrations.

You would have thought that the date would be accurate but there are an amazing number of people out there celebrating birthdays on days which are not their birth dates! One reason is that parents lied about the date of birth to bring the birth date within the limits for registration. These days, birth dates are checked against other lists to confirm their accuracy but that is a recent development. If you are getting one set of birth dates from one source such as a baptism and another set from the certificate have a look at Column 8 on the birth certificate and see how close to the six weeks limit (or only three weeks in the early days) the registration was. There is no such thing as a "late" baptism and therefore less need for parents to massage the truth.

Parents with large families frequently muddle which child was born when especially when the birth dates are close to one another – a second reason why the date of birth is sometimes not accurate.

If there is a time against the date of birth then there may have been more than one child born alive at the birth. If however a mother had twins, one liveborn and one stillborn, then the live born twin will not have a time against the birth. Until 1926 there were no registrations at all of a still born child. Having said that, again the early registrations are not consistent. The registrar in the Eton district did not put the times of births of twins in the registers at all until 1845 while the one in Stoke-on-Trent put times against all the registrations up until about 1850.

If a child lived even for a few seconds there should be both a birth registration and a death registration but I think in the early days that this wasn't always done and sometimes only a death registration can be found.

Place of birth

The place of birth is not terribly helpful in the early registrations. The description is likely to be just the village name although "posh" people with big houses sometimes got their house names even on the early registrations. By 1860 more of the address was commonly in use e.g. I have an 1861 registration in Cirencester which gives the place of birth as Cricklade Street Cirencester. By about 1880 reasonably full addresses were in use.

You need to look at the place of birth against the informant and address in Column 7. If mother has registered and the addresses given in Column 2, and 7 are identical you have probably got mother's address at the time of the birth.

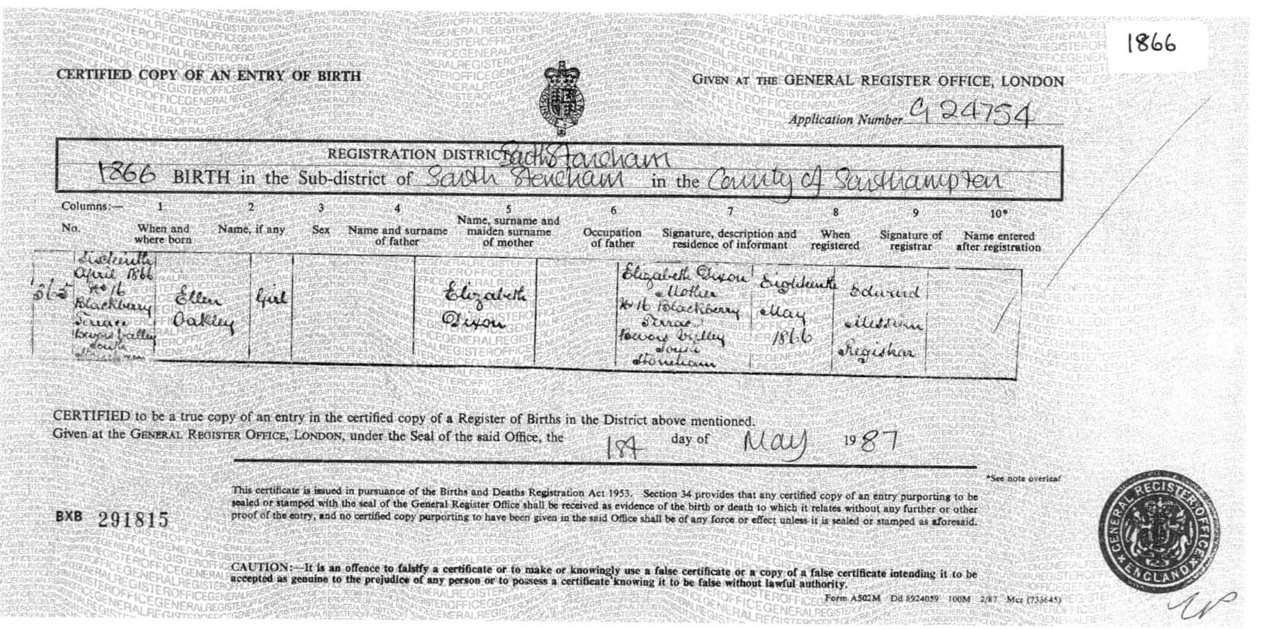

1866

CERTIFIED COPY OF AN ENTRY OF BIRTH

GIVEN AT THE GENERAL REGISTER OFFICE, LONDON

Application Number G 24754

REGISTRATION DISTRICT South Stoneham

1866 BIRTH in the Sub-district of South Stoneham in the County of Southampton

Columns:—	1	2	3	4	5	6	7	8	9	10*
No.	When and where born	Name, if any	Sex	Name and surname of father	Name, surname and maiden surname of mother	Occupation of father	Signature, description and residence of informant	When registered	Signature of registrar	Name entered after registration
365	Sixteenth April 1866 No 16 Blackberry Terrace Bevois Valley South [illegible]	Ellen Oakley	Girl		Elizabeth Dixon		Elizabeth Dixon Mother No 16 Blackberry Terrace Bevois Valley South Stoneham	Eighteenth May 1866	Edward [illegible] Registrar	

CERTIFIED to be a true copy of an entry in the certified copy of a Register of Births in the District above mentioned.
Given at the GENERAL REGISTER OFFICE, LONDON, under the Seal of the said Office, the 18th day of May 1987

BXB 291815

*See note overleaf

This certificate is issued in pursuance of the Births and Deaths Registration Act 1953. Section 34 provides that any certified copy of an entry purporting to be sealed or stamped with the seal of the General Register Office shall be received as evidence of the birth or death to which it relates without any further or other proof of the entry, and no certified copy purporting to have been given in the said Office shall be of any force or effect unless it is sealed or stamped as aforesaid.

CAUTION:—It is an offence to falsify a certificate or to make or knowingly use a false certificate or a copy of a false certificate intending it to be accepted as genuine to the prejudice of any person or to possess a certificate knowing it to be false without lawful authority.

Form A502M Dd 8924059 100M 2/87 Mcr (733645)

GENERAL REGISTER OFFICE ENGLAND

Certificate of Ellen Oakley

This is the certificate of one of my husband's remoter cousins and is a classic case of illegitimacy. No details of father are recorded in Columns 4 and 6. However, there is a pitfall here, because we thought it likely that the father of Elizabeth's baby was a certain Mr Oakley, given the first names of Ellen Oakley Dixon. Subsequent research showed, in fact, that Elizabeth had left her home in Birkenhead and travelled to Southampton to stay with her sister Ellen Oakley (née Dixon). Presumably Elizabeth had named her daughter after her sister. Note that there is a very precise address even though this one dates from 1866.

Ditto for father. But if, for example, you have an illegitimate child born in the workhouse and the workhouse master registered – quite a common occurrence – then you have not got a permanent address for the mother of the child. What you have is the address at which the birth took place – the workhouse – and the address of the informant who lives at the workhouse. In early registrations the mother has probably not travelled far from home to give birth, but even so may have come from several parishes away. In later dates mothers often travelled very long distances from home especially when the baby was going to be adopted and the pregnancy hidden from the rest of the family/village.

Similarly if the mother went to her mother for the birth of a baby she could be quite a long way away from her real home but it will not necessarily show on the registration. What you could have is the address at which the birth took place – grandmothers – and the informant's address which might be another member of the family such as a sister who was present at the birth.

Again, if you are looking for a birth registration and can find one that matches what you were expecting, you have probably found the correct one. If the scenario above applies, however, you could be discounting registrations that are in fact yours.

Column 2 – Forenames

The name(s) entered in Column 2 of a birth certificate is/are the forenames only.

A child can be registered without a first name and even today that is occasionally done. Sometimes that is because – despite nearly nine months plus six weeks to register in – the family has not yet chosen a name. Know the feeling actually – if we had had girls they would have been nameless! Sometimes that is because the baby has already died and the family is registering both the birth and the death and do not name the child. Sometimes this is because the baby is going to be adopted and the mother cannot cope with naming the child – it gives the baby more of an identity and makes it harder for the mother.

Children registered with two first names are frequently called by the second. One of my husband's family had ten sons, all with two first names, and all those that survived without fail were called by the second one. This is fine if somewhere there is an indication that there was a first element not being used but if they marry and are in the census and die as Frederick it is difficult to match that with the birth registration index for William F.

Even more baffling are the people that have a name that bears no resemblance to any of their given names. My favourite of the moment was the man called Nicholas Curry who was always called Harry (You might have to think about that one – give you a clue – try reading it as Hari). My father's half-uncle was registered as Luther but every single further reference to him is to Reuben. That was because his father registered him as Luther and his mother didn't like it and refused to use it so he was always called Reuben. Since we know that was the case it hasn't caused a problem but once you've gone past the oral history stage it can cause great problems.

Where a child was illegitimate with no father's details in the register it is quite common to find a name such as William Johnston in Column 2 which might possibly suggest a surname for the father of the child. However do not assume this is the case until you have confimation from other sources – look at the birth certificates of Ellen Oakley Dixon on page 6 and William Pritchard Love on page 10 to see how easy it is to make a mistake.

Unlike many countries, there is no proscribed list of names from which the parents must choose. The only prohibitions on names are that they must not be blasphemous or obscene. If the parents wish to name their child Humpty Dumpty they can. Similarly there is no proscribed list of spellings for names either so you sometimes get very strange spellings in the name column – perhaps because the parents deliberately choose to spell the names in the most obscure fashion possible to make the child different, (they aren't going to have to go through life spelling it to everyone of course) or even because spelling is not the parent's strong point. I have seen a registration for a baby girl with the name of Epiphany – except that mother spelt it Appifanny and on another occasion a boy as Jamie – but spelt Jammie.

Names can be very helpful in placing an approximate age on someone. A surprising number of people have a second name that is the place of a famous battle or after a soldier hero or politician or pop star or whatever.

For the surname of the child you have to look at Column 4 or Column 6 where the parents names are recorded .

Column 3 – Sex

Now we are beginning to get to the *really* interesting parts! Before 1969 the sex of the child was denoted by boy or girl and after that date by male or female. And you would think that was the end of the matter but you have to remember that the information is only as accurate as the person giving it makes it.

There have been mistakes made in the sex of the child. It can always be a problem if the child is being given a name which does not denote a sex e.g. Alex. Would you know automatically what sex a child named Storm or Aston is? And if the parents go in for very obscure names from mythology or strange first names which are part of the family tradition it can be even more difficult. Especially where parents are illiterate and cannot read the register for themselves to check it is right, it is quite possible for mistakes to be made in any part of the information including the sex of the child.

Sometimes is quite possible to be mistaken about the sex of a baby. I know it doesn't sound likely, but believe me it happens. I have an acquaintance who proudly phoned everyone to say his first child was a boy and then had to phone everyone again the next day to say – oops – actually it's a girl!

And on very rare occasions there are children born for whom it is very difficult indeed to ascertain the sex.

On both my husband's side of the family and mine there is a case of a child baptised as one sex but registered and named as the other. In one case it is fairly clear what has happened. The parents of the child were called John and Ann and the male child was registered and called John after his father but was baptised as a female child Ann after her mother. As a baptism is often written into the baptismal register sometime after the event it is possible that the minister could only remember that the child was named after one of its parents and got it wrong or the parents were not too sober at the christening!

In the other case there is at least some information because sixty years later the sex and name had to be determined in law because of a court case over a will (or lack of it). It would seem as though the first child of a marriage was born on 15th Nov 1842 and registered as a male, Joseph. However, by the time of the baptism in June the following year the child was named as a female called Mary. Each of the surviving five sisters and brothers of Mary had to swear that they had never had a brother called Joseph and that Mary was the eldest surviving

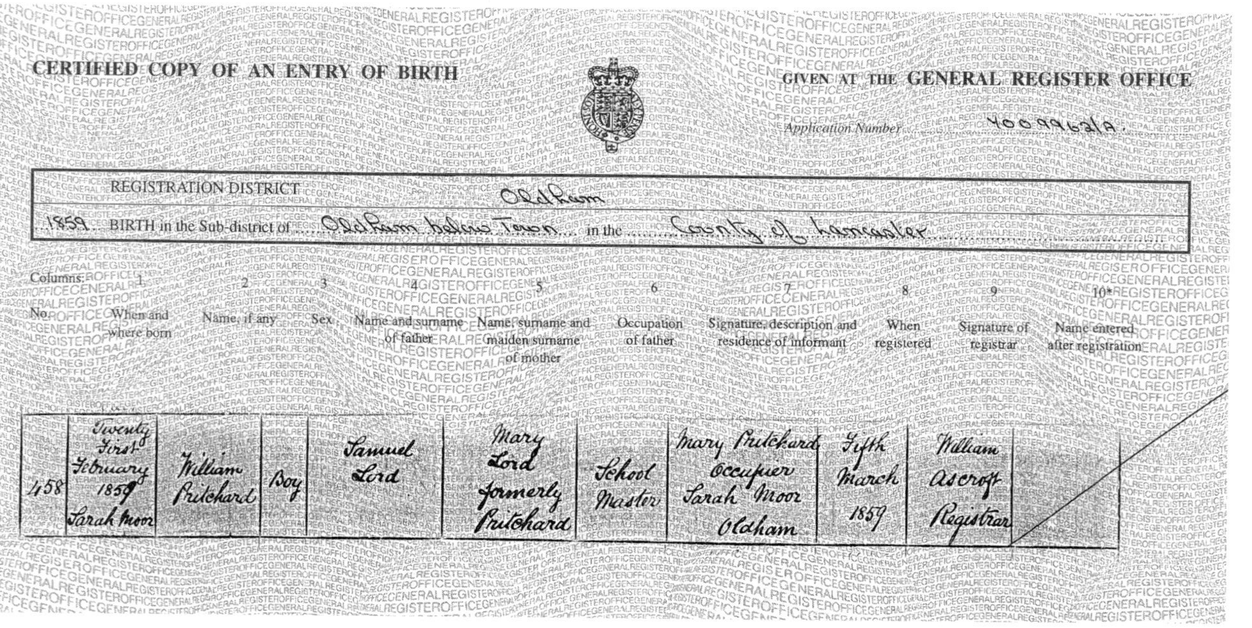

CERTIFIED COPY OF AN ENTRY OF BIRTH

GIVEN AT THE GENERAL REGISTER OFFICE

Application Number 40099621A.

REGISTRATION DISTRICT Oldham

1859 BIRTH in the Sub-district of Oldham below Town in the County of Lancaster

Columns: 1		2	3	4	5	6	7	8	9	10*
No.	When and where born	Name, if any	Sex	Name and surname of father	Name, surname and maiden surname of mother	Occupation of father	Signature, description and residence of informant	When registered	Signature of registrar	Name entered after registration
458	Twenty First February 1859 Sarah Moor	William Pritchard	Boy	Samuel Lord	Mary Lord formerly Pritchard	School Master	Mary Pritchard Occupier Sarah Moor Oldham	Fifth March 1859	William Ascroft Registrar	

Certificate of William Pritchard Love

Note the vague address shown in Column 1. The forenames in Column 2 would suggest that Pritchard might be a family name, which this time is confirmed in Column 5. The occupier of the property has signed in Column 7 and the surname Pritchard suggests a relative – in fact the maternal grandmother. It is always worth chasing up informants who are occupiers because they could well be a long lost branch of the family. This is a case where you do not know where the parents of William were living – you have the grandmothers address only. Reproduced by kind permission of Jenny Bartlett

child of their parents. (Mary was definitely female as she married a man and had a family). It was not possible to squeeze two pregnancies in to the time scale and there was no death and no family recollection of a Joseph. Why both the sex of the child and the name were wrong was never established.

So if you have someone in the family who seems to have been born but never died or married and you have another one of the opposite sex of roughly the same age for whom you cannot find a birth registration ... maybe?

Column 4 – Father's Name

There is still a fundamental difference between the way children born inside and outside of marriage are registered because there are still differences in law between the two. For example inheritance was affected by legitimacy in the past and the nationality of a child still may be.

Whether father is entered in the register depends on two factors – were the couple married when the baby was born (always entered) or, if not, the date the registration was made (maybe, maybe not).

The early registrations between 1837 and approximately 1850 are a little mixed. The Act of Parliament of 1836 reads "And it be enacted that the father or mother of every child born in England ... shall within 42 days next after the day of every such birth give information upon being requested so to do to the Registrar, according to the best of his or her knowledge and belief of the several particulars hereby required to be known and registered touching the birth of such child provided always that it shall not be necessary to register the name of any father of a bastard child."

Now some registrars interpreted that quite freely and put father in even where the couple were not married and only mother or someone else was signing the register and some did not allow fathers details to be entered in the register. By about 1850 the situation had been clarified and the instructions read quite clearly "No putative father is to be allowed to sign an entry in the character of 'Father'." From that time, therefore there are two kinds of entries in the register:

1 Where the parents were married to one another, father's details must be entered in the register and only one parent will sign the register (or some other informant).

2 Where the parents were not married to one another there will be blanks in Column 4 (father's name) and Column 6 (his occupation).

This situation lasted until the Registration Act of 1875 where the instruction read "The putative father of an illegitimate child cannot be required as father to give information respecting the birth. The name, surname and occupation of the putative father of an illegitimate child must not be entered except at the joint request of the father and mother; in which case both the father and mother must sign the entry as informants". There are therefore three kinds of entry after this Act:

1 Described above.
2 Described above.
3 Where the parents are not married to one another but both attended the register office together, (this is called a joint registration), father's details are entered in Column 4 and Column 6 and both parents sign. Looked at a different way – after 1875 if both parents have signed in Column 7 regardless of what names they are using then the parents were not married to one another at the time of the birth of the child.

This situation lasted until 1953 when the same three entries could still be made but there were other ways in which father when not married to mother could be included in the entry without being present to sign but I don't think this later period will be of interest to most family historians so I haven't included it. If a mother was widowed before the birth of her legitimate baby the entry will show (deceased) after father's occupation.

The child will take its surname from that of father in Column 4 where the parents were married and from mother in Column 5 if they were not married and father's name is not entered. The child could take either surname if it was a joint entry and both mother's and father's surnames are shown but are different.

The name given for the father is the name he was known by at the time of the birth of the baby. These days if the father has changed his name between his own birth and that of his child he could be entered in the register as e.g. John SMITH formerly known as John GRAY but that was not the case until fairly recently. If a man adopted his stepfather's name or that of the family who brought him up or used his fathers name even though only mother's was shown on his birth certificate you are going to have a problem going back any more generations. You have to remember that until the recent advances in fertility treatment – the maternity of the child has never been in doubt but the paternity is known only to the mother! Seriously – it is the reason why the mother has always been the prime informant for the birth of a child ever since 1837.

Column 5 – Mother's Name

Column 5 of a birth certificate shows the name, and previous names if any, of the mother of the baby. There are several combinations of name possible. If a woman has never been married there will be a sole entry for her name e.g. Martha Robinson. If a woman has been married once there will be two names shown for her e.g. Martha Robinson formerly Wheeler. If a woman has been married more than once all the previous names shown will be e.g. Martha Robinson late Wheeler formerly Gregory. If a woman has been married, all previous names should be shown whether the baby being registered was legitimate or not.

In later records it is possible to find a mother registered along the lines of e.g. Margaret Blinco otherwise Margaret Joel. This shows that she was using a name to which she didn't have legal entitlement e.g. she was living with someone called Blinco and using his name but was not married to him. Margaret Blinco otherwise Margaret Joel formerly Smith would show that she started life as a Smith, married and became Joel and was now living with someone and using his name of Blinco.

This information is correct for registrations up to 1st April 1969 when the format of the registers changed.

It is important to remember that the definition of the maiden surname in registration is *not* the surname of a woman at birth but is the surname she was using at the first marriage. So someone who was born Ellen Hudson but who had changed her name to her stepfather's surname of Culshaw before she was married would have a maiden surname of Culshaw not Hudson. The reason for that is when tracing back , the next step would be to find the marriage of a child's parents and so it is necessary to look for the names used at marriage. The marriage certificate should show the natural fathers' name not the stepfathers and so therefore you would have the birth name. That's the theory! The practice is often different as we know.

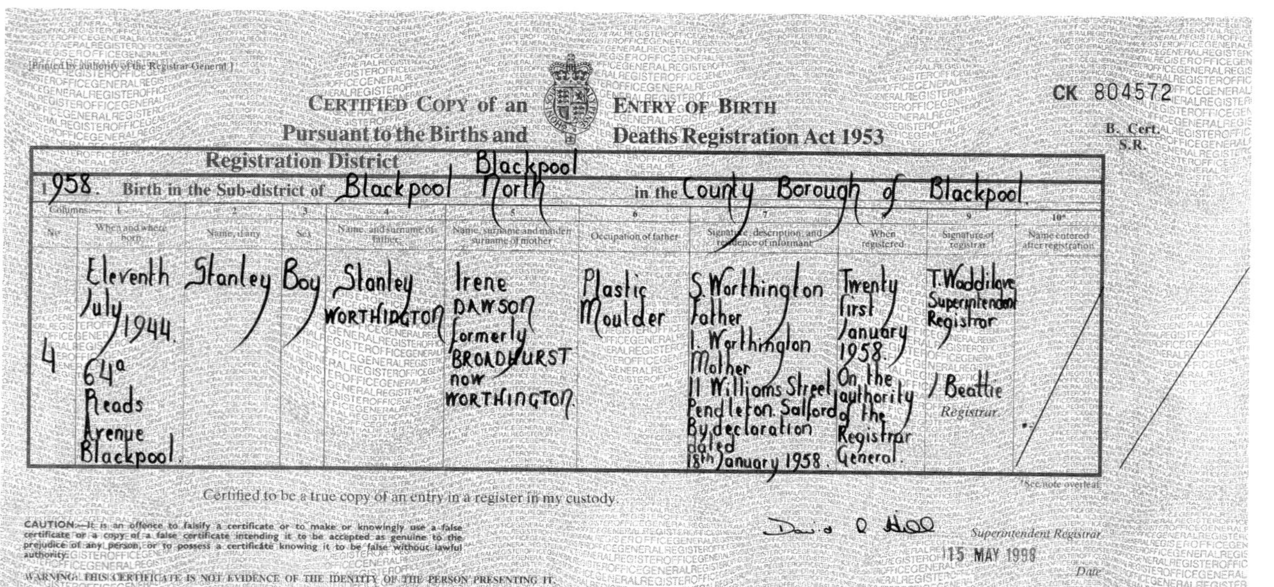

[Printed by authority of the Registrar General.]

CK 804572

B. Cert. S.R.

CERTIFIED COPY of an ENTRY OF BIRTH

Pursuant to the Births and Deaths Registration Act 1953

Registration District Blackpool

1958. Birth in the Sub-district of Blackpool North in the County Borough of Blackpool.

Columns:— 1 No.	When and where born	2 Name, if any	3 Sex	4 Name and surname of father	5 Name, surname and maiden surname of mother	6 Occupation of father	7 Signature, description and residence of informant	8 When registered	9 Signature of registrar	10* Name entered after registration
4	Eleventh July 1944. 64a Reads Avenue Blackpool.	Stanley	Boy	Stanley WORTHINGTON	Irene DAWSON formerly BROADHURST now WORTHINGTON.	Plastic Moulder	S. Worthington Father I. Worthington Mother 11 Williams Street Pendleton, Salford By declaration dated 18th January 1958.	Twenty first January 1958. On the authority of the Registrar General.	T. Waddilove Superintendent Registrar / Beattie Registrar.	

*See note overleaf.

Certified to be a true copy of an entry in a register in my custody.

David Q Hill Superintendent Registrar

15 MAY 1998 Date

CAUTION:—It is an offence to falsify a certificate or to make or knowingly use a false certificate or a copy of a false certificate intending it to be accepted as genuine to the prejudice of any person, or to possess a certificate knowing it to be false without lawful authority.

WARNING: THIS CERTIFICATE IS NOT EVIDENCE OF THE IDENTITY OF THE PERSON PRESENTING IT.

The certificate of Stanley Worthington

This is a re-registration shown by the huge discrepancy between the date of birth and the date of registration, and the words "On the authority of the Registrar General" with the date. Mother's details in Column 5 shows that she started life as Broadhurst, married and became Dawson (the name she was known by at the time of the birth) but was using the surname Worthington at the time of the re-registration. Because the parents were now living in Salford, the birth was re-registered by declaration – ie they went to the Salford registrar who posted the details to the Blackpool registrar to put in his register. Both the superintendent registrar and the registrar have signed in Column 9 because the registration is more than 3 months after the event. Reproduced by kind permission of Stanley Worthington.

Married women never apparently had an occupation! Being a wife and mother was all the occupation they were allowed (and this was not altered until a few years ago when women were finally allowed to have an occupation shown against their name and only since April 1996 has there been a dedicated space for a mother's occupation). However, mothers of illegitimate children had an occupation shown – one of the few compensations for illegitimacy.

All the problems associated with changes of name for one reason or another were covered in the section on the fathers name.

Column 6 – Father's Occupation

Column 4 and Column 6 go together. If there is no father shown in Column 4 then there will be no occupation shown in Column 6. If there is a father shown in Column but a line drawn through Column 6 it means that the father did not have an occupation or perhaps was not employed at the time of the registration or the informant did not know what father did.

Only paid employment is shown and, as in the census, men only had legal and respectable jobs so you won't find pimp or burglar! On the other hand, before this century they probably had a more meaningful occupation than the ones you get at present – blacksmith, shepherd, coalporter or whatever rather than company director (owns his own windowcleaning company) or office administrator (files bits of paper). Informants can be modest about occupations as well as aggrandising them.

Labourer might mean totally unskilled – heaving stuff about in a market – but could equally mean a quite specific skill e.g. many 'ag labs' (agricultural labourers) were quite specialised workers such as hay trussers.

Especially in the past, occupations would show status such as "of independent means".

If a father of a legitimate baby had died before his baby was born then Column 6 would read something on the lines of "Railway worker (deceased)."

Column 7 – Signature, Description and Residence of the Informant

Signature

Once the entry has been checked by the informant, he or she signs in Column 7 – their usual signature. If the informant can't sign their name then they make a mark and the registrar completes it with the words "The mark of ……." If you see this on a certificate warning bells should start to ring. It means that the informant has been unable to check the information for himself/herself and the registrar has done the best possible. Especially where a family has a name that is unusual in the locality where they are now living and where they have a strong accent, it is going to be luck if the registrar hits on the correct spelling of it. After all how many of you would spell Kirkcudbright correctly if you did not already know how it was pronounced and spelt and you had someone in front of you saying Kecoobree?

If someone can sign their name but in a different script then they sign in Chinese or Arabic or whatever and the registrar writes "The signature of ……". Same problem really – the informants probably can't check for themselves that the information is correct.

A signature does not necessarily mean that the informant could read. Many people learnt to write their name but nothing else. In a way this is worse because you don't know if they could read or not!

Description of informant

The current list of eligible informants reads, in order of preference:

1 In all cases – mother
2 Father – if he is married to mother
3 A person present at the birth
4 The owner or occupier of the house or institution
5 The person in charge of the child

After 1875 a joint registration could be made by the mother and father of the baby together if they were not married. Before that father's details could not be given (from about 1850 to 1875) and before that it is a little bit variable, see Column 4.

1 Mother – mother was usually not in doubt although it was not unknown in the past for grandmother to go the register office and register her daughter's illegitimate child as her own.
2 Father – he is the second choice by preference because – by biology alone – mother knows she is the mother and only she really knows (or might do!) who the father is. There is an assumption in law, however, that unless told otherwise, the husband is the father of the baby.
3 Person present at the birth. This covers a wide range of people – could be grandmother, aunt, sister, midwife, neighbour. The more remote they are in kinship from the parents of the baby, the less likely they are to give accurate information.
4 The owner or occupier of the house or institution. This includes the master of the workhouse, matron of a hospital, a relative or friend if the mother had gone to have the baby there, (see the certificate of William Pritchard Love, page 10).
5 The person in charge of the child. This could be the father of an illegitimate child – he could not register as father and have his details as father included but he could do the registration. It could be the master of the workhouse if an unmarried mother died in childbirth – or equally any vague relative or kind neighbour who took the baby in.

These days it is pretty rare for anyone other than mother or father or both to register although all the other categories are very occasionally used to effect a registration if mother and/or father are not available for whatever reason e.g. I have seen "in charge of the child" in a registration where father of the baby was not known and mother was too mentally disabled to be capable of doing the registration.

The address of the informant. Remember that if a mother has a baby away from her own home and does not do the registration, you do not have an address for her. Addresses can be very vague before about 1880 – often just the name of the town or village is all that is given (see the certificate of Ellen Oakley Dixon, page 6).

In 1837 the list included numbers **1**, **2**, **3** and **4** and by 1875 the list looks much as today.

After 1875 it became possible for parents whose child was born some distance away from their normal home address, to go into their nearest

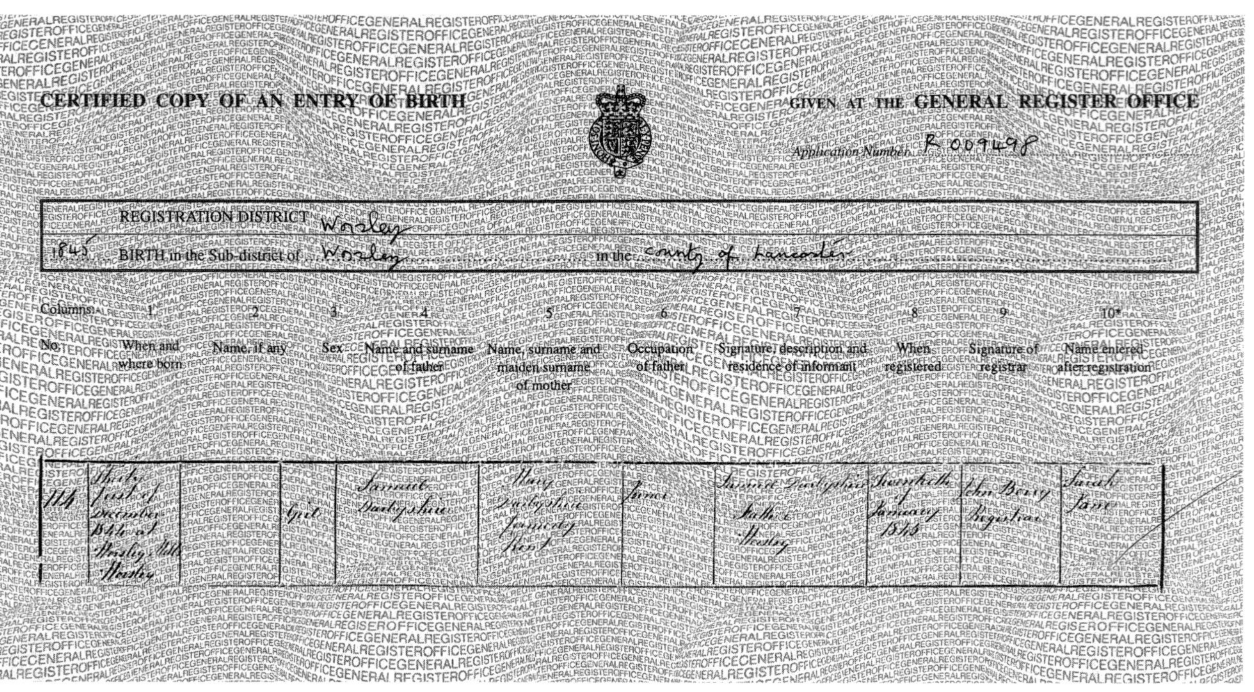

CERTIFIED COPY OF AN ENTRY OF BIRTH — GIVEN AT THE GENERAL REGISTER OFFICE

Application Number R009498

REGISTRATION DISTRICT Worsley

1845 BIRTH in the Sub-district of Worsley in the county of Lancaster

Columns:– 1 No.	2 When and where born	3 Name, if any	4 Sex	5 Name and surname of father	6 Name, surname and maiden surname of mother	7 Occupation of father	8 Signature, description and residence of informant	9 When registered	10 Signature of registrar	10* Name entered after registration
114	Thirty first of December 1844 at Worsley Mill Worsley		Girl	Samuel Darbyshire	Mary Darbyshire formerly Kent	Joiner	Samuel Darbyshire Father Worsley	Twentieth of January 1845	John Berry Registrar	Sarah Jane

Certificate of Sarah Jane Darbyshire

Note the blank for the child's names in Column 2 and the name entered after registration in Column 10. From 1926 Column 10 would also carry the words "by baptism on ......" or "by certificate of naming dated ......". This is another registration which appears in the next quarter's indexes – indeed in the next year. Reproduced by kind permission of Mike Longworth.

registrar instead of having to attend at the register office in the district where the child was born. The details were taken by the registrar in their home district and posted to the registrar where the birth had taken place. If this has been done, there is no signature in the registrar by the informant. Instead the registrar doing the registration will have copied the signature into the registrar and written "by declaration dated ......" after it (see the certificate of Stanley Worthington, page 14).

Column 8 – Date of Registration

This is very relevant to the indexes because birth, death and marriage indexes are compiled by the date of registration *not* the date of the event (in marriages these two dates are usually the same but can be very different in births and deaths). So a baby born on e.g. 25th November 1851 that was not registered until 2nd January 1852 would be indexed in the March quarter for 1852 not the December quarter for 1851, (see the certificate of Sarah Jane Darbyshire page 18)

In the early days the parents had three weeks to register in and could not register at all after three months. After a while this was changed to six weeks to register in, a late registration could be made up to a year after the birth if the superintendent took the information and signed the register too, and registration could not take place after one year without reference to GRO. Once the delay was this long then proof of the event had to be provided by other parties who knew of this event e.g. midwife or doctor or siblings alive at the time and able to recall the event. Even now, if it is not possible to provide the proof and/or the people who can attest to the truth of the event it is not possible to register and there are people walking around today with no birth certificate.

It means, therefore, that a birth registered very late could be in the indexes a whole year later or more than expected. It is also relevant in that there were penalties for late registrations that were quite severe in the beginning and rather than get into trouble parents would "adjust" the date of birth to fall within the specified time for registration. If you have a discrepancy between a date of birth on a certificate and one given on a baptismal certificate, have a look at the date of registration. If it is very close to the six weeks, it is quite likely that the parents didn't tell the truth at registration but did at baptism where there were no penalties. There were no checks on the dates of birth given by the informant until well into this century.

Column 9 – Signature of Registrar

This is not particularly relevant unless you have an ancestor who was a registrar! If the registrar AND the superintendent registrar have both signed in Column 9 then there was something unusual about the registration – such as a late one or a re-registration of a birth. There is usually a large difference between the date of birth and the date of registration in these cases.

Column 10 – Name Given After Initial Registration

This is for the entry of a name given after initial registration. This relates to the fact that before civil registration, the recording of the major life events was in the hands of the church and especially of course of the established church (Church of England). There was tremendous resistance to civil registration by the established church who felt (rightly as it happened) that people would stop baptising their children if they had an alternative piece of legal paper in a civil registration.

If a child was registered without a first name and was then baptised, or if a child was registered with forenames that were changed at baptism – because baptism was in place before civil registration and was considered more important – then the facility was given to change the first names (but *not* the surname). These days the baptism must take place within one year of the date of registration but the alteration can be made to the register at any time once the baptism has been completed.

The importance of this is that very often a child had a name changed by baptism but the civil registration was not corrected. That means that the name used by the child will not match the indexes, which are amended if a space 10 correction is made. At baptism the names made be altered in order, changed in spelling, new ones put in, names taken out or changed totally. These days there is a facility for names to be changed without baptism because of course many people are of other faiths or do not go to church. If you cannot find the correct registration for an ancestor, it might be worth looking at other registrations with the wrong name but in the right place and at the right time, and also looking for a baptism (see the certificate of Sarah Jane Darbyshire, page 18)

Applying for your birth certificate

Once you have found the probable birth registration, you can apply for the certificate in one of two ways. If you are at the GRO and can complete one of the proper forms, it is probably as fast and as convenient to apply directly to GRO remembering to quote all the relevant information asked for.

On the back of the form it is possible to specify further information such as parents' names, or occupations. This is a bit of a mixed blessing. If you tick this box, then you will only receive your certificate if there is an exact match to your data. If, for example, you state that father is a blacksmith and his occupation on the birth certificate only states labourer, even though all other details match, you will not be sent your certificate and half the cost will be kept by GRO for the work done to locate the possible entry.

If you are looking at indexes elsewhere, then you might prefer to apply directly to the Superintendent Registrar of the appropriate registration district. If you do this, then there is absolutely no point in quoting the GRO reference – this is for the national indexes remember. Local register offices index their registers in quite a different fashion. You would need to quote the name of the child, the registration district, the year of birth and the quarter and any other information known e.g. names of parents.

A large registration district was divided into two or more sub-districts, e.g. the Eton Registration district in 1837 had three – the Eton, Burnham, and Iver sub-districts. Each birth had to be registered in its correct sub-district. Applications for a birth certificate can sometimes take quite a while to get to the correct current registration district; e.g. if you find a birth in the December quarter 1852 Eton district and ask where Eton registrations are held you will be told to apply to the Windsor and Maidenhead Register Office (because that is where current Eton registrations go). However, none of the Eton registrations before 1974 are held there – and most of them are at Slough so the application will be passed on to Slough. Slough only has two out of the three Eton sub-districts however, and once a search has been made of those it will be passed to Chiltern and South Bucks. Not surprising then if your certificate takes some time to get to you!

Adoptions

There were no formal or legal arrangements for adoptions until 1926. From that time an adoption register has been kept, which gives the new name of an adopted child but there is no link back to the name with which the child was originally registered. Before 1926 many children were brought up in families that were not their own. If they kept their own surname, then they are traceable, but many children took the surname of the relative, neighbour, friend who brought them up and then it is extremely difficult to find the original birth registration.

Stillbirths

There was no registration of stillbirths until 1926. Registers of stillbirths are sent to the General Register Office when complete, so there is no record in the local register office, there are no indexes to stillbirth registers and the certificates from stillbirths are not issued to those doing genealogy.

Re-registrations

Before 1926, a child born out of wedlock could only have the father's details in the register if both parents went together to register (a joint registration). Once registered, a child could not be re-registered even if the parents subsequently married. In 1926 the law concerning illegitimacy was changed, so that a child born before the parents married was subsequently legitimised on the marriage. It therefore became necessary to introduce re-registrations, so that a new entry could be made showing the child as that of the marriage.

In these cases, there will be two registrations for the child – the original one at the time of the birth and a second one which could be any number of years later depending on when the parents subsequently married, and when they got round to doing the re-registration. If you find an entry in the indexes which is yours and you apply for it and the child was in fact re-registered at a later date, it will always be the second, later registration that will be sent to you.

You can usually pick up a re-registration by noticing the big difference between the date of birth and the date of registration, and by the words "on the authority of the Registrar General" in Column 8 with the date of registration. Note however, that a very late birth registration (over a year after the date of birth) will look the same.

DEATH CERTIFICATES

Introduction

It is important to remember that people do not necessarily die in their own beds! It is quite possible that your ancestor was away visiting or working and died away from home and so will be registered in an unexpected registration district.

Heading

The heading section is identical to those on Birth Certificates and can be found on page 1.

Entry Number

This is found in the first column and could be anything between 1 and 500 in the early registers. Remember that there were five entries to the page and they will all have the identical GRO reference. You might find two members of the same family with the same reference number in the same quarter – perhaps because two children have died of the same childhood disease such as diptheria, or you could have a mother and new baby dying or two members of the family dying together in an accident. Or it could be coincidence!

Column 1 Date and Place of Death

Most deaths are registered within a day or two of the date of death. A death certified by a doctor should be registered within five days of the death and a death certified after a post-mortem within 14 days. If there has been an accident or suspicious circumstances or an unexplained death and an inquest has been held, the lag between death and registration could be as long as a year although in the past the delay was still only a couple of weeks. The death is not registered until the inquest has been held.

If the death being registered is that of a baby that lived for less than 24 hours, then these days the hours or minutes that the baby lived would be shown with words such as "Aged 2 hours" or "Aged 11 minutes" but I do not think this was common practice in the last century.

If a body has been found and the precise date of death cannot be ascertained then there may be wording such as "Dead body found on ......" or "On or about the twelfth June ......". If someone is taken ill but is dead by the time they have reached hospital there could be the wording "Found dead on arrival at ......" but again this is a more modern occurrence.

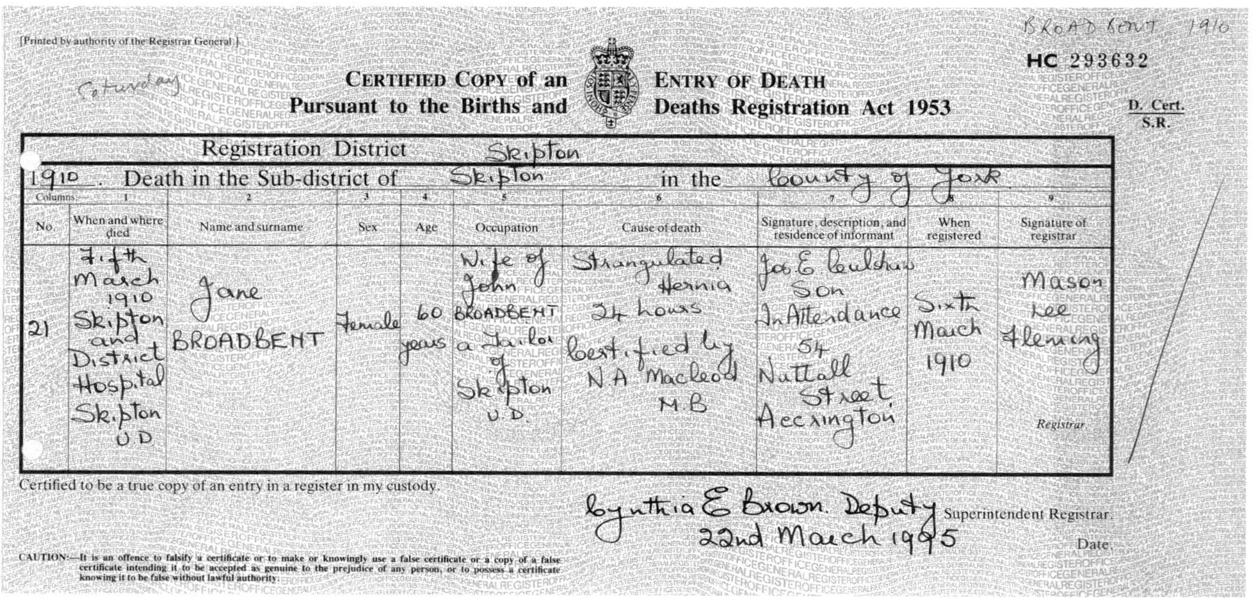

[Printed by authority of the Registrar General.]

BROADBENT 1910

HC 293632

Saturday

CERTIFIED COPY of an ENTRY OF DEATH
Pursuant to the Births and Deaths Registration Act 1953

D. Cert.
S.R.

Registration District Skipton

1910. Death in the Sub-district of Skipton in the County of York

No.	When and where died	Name and surname	Sex	Age	Occupation	Cause of death	Signature, description, and residence of informant	When registered	Signature of registrar
21	Fifth March 1910 Skipton and District Hospital Skipton U.D	Jane BROADBENT	Female	60 years	Wife of John BROADBENT a Tailor of Skipton U.D.	Strangulated Hernia 24 hours Certified by N.A. Macleod M.B	Jos E. Coulshaw Son In Attendance 54 Nuttall Street Accrington	Sixth March 1910	Mason Lee Fleming Registrar

Certified to be a true copy of an entry in a register in my custody.

Cynthia E Brown. Deputy Superintendent Registrar.
22nd March 1995 Date.

CAUTION:—It is an offence to falsify a certificate or to make or knowingly use a false certificate or a copy of a false certificate intending it to be accepted as genuine to the prejudice of any person, or to possess a certificate knowing it to be false without lawful authority.

Notes on certificate of Jane Broadbent

This death certificate of my great grandmother gives her husband's name and occupation, but no address for either Jane or husband as she died in hospital and her son has registered. The different surname for her son indicates a previous marriage. A doctor has certified the death.

The place of death could be anywhere! Note that you do not necessarily have the address of the deceased. Column 1 is the place where the death occurred and Column 7 gives the address of the person registering the death but nowhere is there a column which gives the specific address of the deceased. If someone dies away from home and the death is registered by someone other than the wife or husband of the deceased you do not have the home address of the deceased (see the certificate of Jane Broadbent page 24).

The address shown may not give you the precise nature of the building. Institutions such as prisons or pyschiatric hospitals have alternative addresses e.g. 24 London Road which are used when someone is born or dies in them but this is fairly modern use. Older certificates will have the exact description of the institution shown.

As with the births, the address may be very vague in the early days of registration. It might simply say "Skipton" or "Enfield". By the 1860s there is often a street given and by the 1880s a fairly precise address would be given. If therefore you have an imprecise address e.g. King Street given when you would expect a precise address you are probably looking at the true place of death – i.e. the person really did die on King Street rather than in a house on King Street (see page 36).

Column 2 – Name and Surname of the Deceased

This is the name by which they were known at the date of death. If, therefore, someone started life with a different name but by usage has come to be called something else you will not find any reference to the original name on older certificates. Sometimes people have dropped a first name so that a child named John Stanley FRANCIS at birth might only be known as Stanley FRANCIS by the time they die. Where a child was illegitimate at birth and only registered with mother's details they could only have mother's surname on the birth certificate. However, they might well be known all their life by their father's surname so, for example, someone with a birth certificate of Samuel HOLLOWAY might be registered at death as Samuel STEWART.

A baby that has died might not be given a first name and the death registration would simply show ——— GREEN and all registrations where the information is not known will have lines drawn through the relevant spaces.

Sometimes someone would be found dead on the road or in a house and no-one knew very much information about them – even today this still happens and in the past when people carried much less in the way of paperwork about themselves it happened more frequently.

These days a person is frequently registered in more than one name so that all previous names would be shown. My two favourite examples were the man who was known as something on the lines of Charles WELLINGTON who was born with a name something like Abraham LEVI and the other was the man who had changed his surname to that of his stepfather when his Police Sergeant had taken him on one side and suggested gently that he was never going to go far in the police force going into court and being named PC Hogsflesh! There are a multitude of reasons why someone should change their name between birth and death – but it doesn't help you much when you are trying to do your family history.

Column 3 – Sex

The fourth column (after entry number, date and place of death, and name) shows the sex of the deceased. This is shown as male or female and although occasionally mistakes are made in this column it is usually obvious from the rest of the information in the other columns if a mistake has been made and has not been corrected at the time.

Column 4 – Age

The column next to this shows the age of the deceased at the date of death. This column must be viewed with a great deal of suspicion! Only if other evidence proves this correct should it be taken to be so. It is best to use it as a starting guide to give you some idea of how old the person was but no more.

There are two reasons why this information is likely to be incorrect. The first is – that the information is not being given by the person to whom it relates! It is being given by someone else – possibly a relative of the deceased – and the more remote the relationship, the more vague will be the information. Where the information is being given by the master of the workhouse, or the neighbour who was sitting with the dying person, the less likely it is to be accurate. I never fail to be amazed by the people who do not know their own dates and places of birth let alone that of their parents but then not everyone is a rabid family historian!

The other reason why the information might not be correct is because the deceased person has lied about it for most of their life or just did not know themselves when they were born and how old they were. Especially in the early days of registration, it was not necessary for people to know exactly how old they were – after all there was no compulsory schooling, no old age pension and so on where it is important to know the date of birth. Many people "adjusted" their ages at one point in their life for whatever reason and thereafter kept to their new age. The sorts of situation would be where a couple under the age of 21 would lie about their age (or one of them would) so that they could get married without parent's consent, or a man or a woman might lose or gain a few years so that the differences in age between themselves and a partner might not appear so big. A man might lie to get into the army (or avoid it!). In large families, especially where children have died and later children have been given the same name as an earlier one, the parents themselves would forget how old their own children were and when they were born.

Column 5 – Occupation

The sixth column on the certificate is for the occupation of the deceased. What is shown will depend on the sex of the deceased, marital status and age, and the date at which the registration is being made.

A man of working age should have his occupation shown. In the last century most men had to work for as long as possible and could still be working at any age. It is possible that an occupation may be given simply as retired (which would imply that they had financial resources from other income), or it may say something on the lines of "not in gainful employment" or "out of employment" or similar for someone too old or too sick to work or who had lost a job during periods of recession. A wealthy person might simply have "Independent" shown but this should not be taken to be the truth until other sources confirm it.

The occupation shown is only the last one that the deceased had which may not give the true picture – for example, a man might be a blacksmith most of his life but towards the end of his working life he might not be able to continue this and be shown only as a labourer on the death certificate.

A single woman might have her occupation shown. Equally there might be simply a blank or for a woman from a wealthy background (even well into

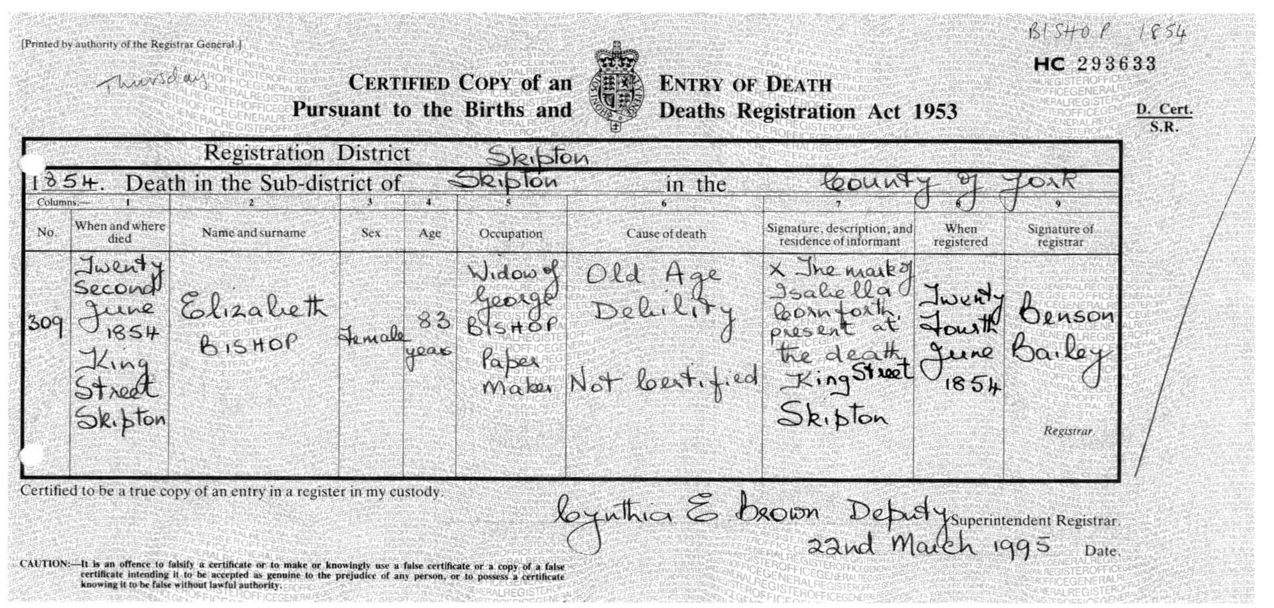

[Printed by authority of the Registrar General.]

Thursday

BISHOP 1854

HC 293633

CERTIFIED COPY of an ENTRY OF DEATH
Pursuant to the Births and Deaths Registration Act 1953

D. Cert.
S.R.

Registration District Skipton

1854. Death in the Sub-district of Skipton in the County of York

No.	1. When and where died	2. Name and surname	3. Sex	4. Age	5. Occupation	6. Cause of death	7. Signature, description, and residence of informant	8. When registered	9. Signature of registrar
309	Twenty Second June 1854 King Street Skipton	Elizabeth BISHOP	Female	83 years	Widow of George BISHOP Paper Maker	Old Age Debility Not Certified	X The mark of Isabella Cornforth present at the death King Street Skipton	Twenty Fourth June 1854	Benson Bailey Registrar

Certified to be a true copy of an entry in a register in my custody.

Cynthia E Brown Deputy Superintendent Registrar.

22nd March 1995 Date.

CAUTION:—It is an offence to falsify a certificate or to make or knowingly use a false certificate or a copy of a false certificate intending it to be accepted as genuine to the prejudice of any person, or to possess a certificate knowing it to be false without lawful authority.

Notes on certificate of Elizabeth Bishop

The death certificate of my great great grandmother tells you that her husband had predeceased her and gives his occupation. The death was not certified by a doctor. There is no confirmed address for Elizabeth. She died at King Street (note the relatively vague addresses in Columns 1 and 7) and the informant lived at King Street, but Elizabeth could have been nursed away from home. It is possible that she was at the same address as the informant, and that Isabella and Elizabeth were related but at this date no relationship is given for the informant and I have not yet tied Isabella Cornforth into my family tree.

her twenties or more) it might say "daughter of ...... (name of father) ...... (his occupation)".

For a wife or widow – her occupation was considered to be being married to her husband! So there will not be any reference to her paid employment (and a vast number of women did work) but it will say "wife (or widow) of ...... (husband's name) ...... (his occupation)". So you cannot tell from this whether a woman had been working – even when they held down professional jobs as they might have done towards the end of the last century and into this one. Married women were not shown as having an occupation until 1969 (see certificates of Jane Broadbent page 24 and Elizabeth Bishop page 28).

For a child it will say "Son or daughter of ...... (father's name) ...... (his occupation)". Again there is no reference to the mother until 1969 unless the child was illegitimate in which case it will say "Son or daughter of ...... (mother's name) ...... (her occupation)", (see page 32).

In the first seven or eight years of registration these patterns are very variable and all sorts of variations can be found but by 1845 the registrations appear to be more consistent.

Column 6 – Cause Of Death

This is the really juicy column. Let me start by explaining who might have given the information that you find given as the cause of death. There are basically 4 possible scenarios:

uncertified death;
certification by a doctor;
certification by a post-mortem but without an Inquest;
certification following an inquest.

In the early days of registration all the deaths were uncertified. The informant simply gave the cause as they saw it. And they were probably not far off the truth. You tend to get simple causes such as measles, stroke, gout, childbirth and so on (see the certificate of Elizabeth Bishop page 28).

It is still possible to have a death not certified by a doctor in which case it is still the informant who is supposed to tell the registrar what the cause of death was. If you have a death certificate without the name of a certifiying doctor and it was not a post-mortem or an inquest then you have an uncertified death. They are pretty rare today – but the sort of situation in which you would have an uncertified death would be where a person died at home at the weekend – they had only been treated by the one doctor from their surgery and that doctor went on holiday for a fortnight starting that weekend. In that case there is no other doctor who can legally sign a certificate. The coroner would then be notified – but if he decides after looking into the matter that there is no need for a post-mortem then you would have an uncertified death.

By 1845 most of the causes of death are followed by the word – certified. Where those words are not found then a doctor did not write a certificate of cause of death. Plenty of families who had sick and dying relatives would not necessarily have called a doctor to see the patient – after all doctors had to be paid.

By 1875 the cause of death is followed by "Certified by ...... (name of doctor) ...... (doctor's qualifications)" in which case the doctor in attendance on the deceased in his last illness has signed a medical certificate of cause of death. This tends then to be in medical jargon e.g. myocardial infarction (a layman would have said heart attack) or cerebrovascular accident (stroke). A doctor is only qualified to sign if he has been in attendance on the deceased in his last illness AND has either seen the deceased within 14 days of his death or saw the deceased after death. If there is no doctor who qualifies under these restrictions then the death must be notified to the coroner (see certificate of Jane Broadbent page 24).

When a death has been notified to the coroner, that coroner may take one of two actions. If the coroner is satisfied with the cause of death and the circumstances immediately before the death, he may decide to take no further action; in which case the original doctor's certificate will stand. If there is no doctor available who is qualified to sign, or the cause of death is not certain, or the circumstances are open to debate, then the coroner may insist on a post-mortem (and the relatives will not be able to object to this). If the post-mortem gives a clear cause of death and the circumstances are not suspicious then the death will be registered on a coroner's post-mortem and the certifying person will be given as the coroner or it may just say "post-mortem" or "PM".

If there are suspicious circumstances and the death is considered to be due to violence (including self-inflicted) or neglect or unnatural (e.g. someone dying from severe sunstroke or alcoholic poisoning) or from an industrial disease just to name a few possibilities, then there will be an inquest.

Where an inquest has been held it will say so although the wording for this varies through time. A verdict will be given such as natural causes, suicide (or deceased took his own life while of unsound mind), accidental death. If an inquest adjourned has been held and there is no verdict given then someone has been charged with the death. In the past it might name the accused, or say murder by person or persons unknown (see certificate of Kent Reeks page 36).

I am not sure if our family is particularly accident prone but of the relatively few death certificates we have (compared to the birth/marriage ones) we have four inquests. One died in a coal mining accident, one died from natural causes (he swallowed a rabbit bone which festered in the lungs and caused rapid death from infection), one drowned in a canal in February and one died from natural causes (a twisted bowel). All four had considerable newspaper coverage which gave lots of detail you would never get anywhere else. The one who drowned in the canal had poor eyesight, was not known to be depressed, was frequently in the habit of staying away from his lodgings all night to look after his son who had been severely ill, had no marks of violence – and if they had looked for such things in those days I suspect he would have had a high alcohol level in his bloodstream! The presumption was that he had had a few drinks in the local pub on the canal towpath, had either stumbled or missed his path due to his poor eyesight and had gone into the canal where the combination of alcohol and low temperature would have finished him off pretty quickly. Verdict – accidental death. Some of the inquest reports in the local papers towards the end of the last century have the most wonderfully intimate detail. The paperwork created by an inquest can sometimes be found in the County Record Office and it is certainly worth looking for as, again, there is a great deal of extra information. For example, it became quite apparent that when my relative died of the twisted bowel, his widow was obviously under suspicion of poisoning him! Fortunately the post-mortem showed quite clearly the nature of his death.

Once deaths were mostly certified by doctors you tend to get more medical jargon – myocardial infarction, status asthmaticus and so on. As these medical terms have not changed and can be found in medical dictionaries I have not attempted to list them here.

BISHOP
18

CERTIFIED COPY OF AN ENTRY OF DEATH GIVEN AT THE **GENERAL REGISTER OFFICE**

Application Number 4010303.

REGISTRATION DISTRICT Skipton.
1872 DEATH in the Sub-district of Skipton in the County of York.

Columns: No.	1 When and where died	2 Name and surname	3 Sex	4 Age	5 Occupation	6 Cause of death	7 Signature, description and residence of informant	8 When registered	9 Signature of registrar
172	Fourth June 1872 Mount Pleasant Skipton	Lancelot Bishop	Male	3 months	Son of John Bishop a Warper	Tabes Mesenterica Certified	X The mark of Ann Thornton present at the death Mount Pleasant Skipton	Sixth June 1872	Benson Bailey Registrar

Notes on certificate of Lancelot Bishop

This is a typical registration of a child, giving only father's name and occupation. There is no confirmed address for father here, only the address where Lancelot died and the address of the informant. (Lancelot's family were living in Bacup when he was born and when his mother died of TB 10 days after he was born.) Ann Thornton could not write and there is no relationship given to Lancelot (she was his maternal aunt).

Some terms however are no longer in common use and these are some of the more commonly occurring ones:

anasarcap	diffused dropsy in the skin;
apoplexy	stroke or cerebral haemorrhage;
climacteric	vague term meaning something unusually severe has happened e.g. heart attack or stroke;
consumption	TB;
dropsy	accumulation of fluid in any tissue (often a symptom of kidney failure or heart failure)
dyspnoea	difficulty in breathing;
marasmus	always of a small child, meaning generalised failure to thrive (could be from a major heart problem or a congenital disease such as intolerance to certain foods etc.);
phthisis	a form of TB;
scrofula	TB (usually of the lymphatic glands);
syncope	usually associated with a heart problem I thought although my dictionary gives lack of blood to the brain as its meaning;
wasting	as for marasmus.

Many of these causes of death would not be acceptable today. For example, dyspnoea would have to be qualified by something giving the reason for the difficulty in breathing, e.g. pneumonia or asthma.

Column 7 – Signature, description and residence of the informant

This can be one of the most useful parts of a death certificate for family historians. The signature could be made by the informant if they could write their name or it could be a mark. A large "X" and the words "the mark of ......" will be familiar to most of you.

The description of the informant has varied with time. In the early days, the informant was one of the following:

someone present at the death;
someone in attendance;
the occupier of a house;
the master or keeper of an institution.

The person present at the death or in attendance (which meant they had been nursing the deceased or in close contact with them during their illness) was also usually a relative, but the early registrations do not give the relationship of the informant to the deceased.

It is always worth remembering with registrations before 1875 that an informant "present at the death", with a name you might not recognise, could be a married daughter that you have had no information on since she left home, or a granddaughter or grandson, son-in-law or any other relative likely to have a different surname from the deceased (see certificates of Elizabeth Bishop page 28 and Lancelot Bishop page 32).

By 1875 the relationship of the informant to the deceased was given – together with additional qualifications such as "present at the death" or "in attendance". People not related to the deceased but present at the death still qualified, but only "present at the death" would be shown.

The occupier (usually the owner) of a house or institution (usually the master of the workhouse) still qualified but in addition the following had been added:

a person who found the body;
inmate of a house or institution – this was a person living at the same address who knew of the event;
person causing the burial;
person in charge of the body.

A relative of the deceased includes any relation by blood or by marriage so that – apart from the widow(er) of the deceased – daughters and sons, grandchildren, cousins, sons- or daughters-in-law, brothers- or sisters-in-law, second cousins, uncles, aunts, nephews and nieces, stepchildren and stepparents all qualify. The early registration make no distinction between relatives by blood or by marriage so, for example, it will say brother whether it is a blood brother or a brother-in-law.

A common-law wife or husband has no status in law for registration purposes and would be unable to register a death of a partner unless they qualified in some other way such as being present at the death. That doesn't stop people lying about their marital status of course! Nor are godchildren or godparents qualified to register.

Someone present at the death could simply have been the person who made a living by sitting with the dying and laying them out after death, or a close friend or neighbour and is not necessarily a relative.

The more remote the relationship to the deceased, the less likely it is that the information they have given is accurate. This is even more true when the master of the workhouse has registered a death as the occupier of the institution where the death took place.

Note that someone whose qualification is "causing the burial or cremation..." is NOT the undertaker. This is the person who is giving the instructions to the undertaker – or in the past – was doing the funeral arrangements themselves. Note also that the executor of a will does not qualify to register unless they are the ones making the funeral arrangements.

When an inquest has taken place then the informant will be the coroner and there will be no signature as such. The column will read something on the lines of "Information received from Thomas Griffin Coroner for the City of Westminster". Later on the date of the Inquest might be given (see certificate of Kent Reeks page 36).

The residence of the informant will vary from just a town or village name in the early registrations to a fuller address. If you think you have a married daughter or sister or other long lost relative doing a registration you should have a name and address – enough to look on a census, or to look for a marriage. We found a sister of the main line registering the death of her 90-year-old mother in 1872 – 60 years after the only other time we had found her on her baptism. So once you have the main tree established – don't neglect your death certificates – they can lead to all sorts of further good family history material.

Column 8 – Date of Registration

This is normally very close to the date of death – or even the day of the death itself. Even today only five days is allowed for a death registration, or fourteen if a coroner's post-mortem is required. An Inquest has no time limit.

Occasionally there will be a significant difference between the date of death and the date of registration, e.g. someone may have died without anyone

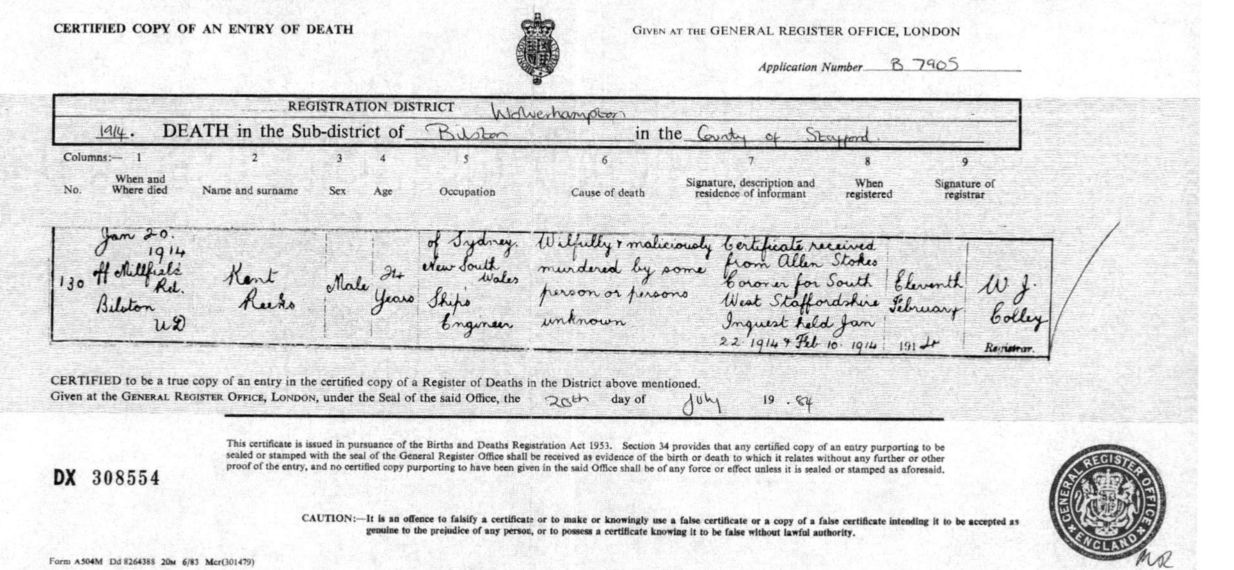

CERTIFIED COPY OF AN ENTRY OF DEATH

GIVEN AT THE GENERAL REGISTER OFFICE, LONDON

Application Number B 7905

REGISTRATION DISTRICT Wolverhampton

1914. DEATH in the Sub-district of Bilston in the County of Stafford.

Columns:—	1	2	3	4	5	6	7	8	9
No.	When and Where died	Name and surname	Sex	Age	Occupation	Cause of death	Signature, description and residence of informant	When registered	Signature of registrar
130	Jan 20. 1914 off Millfields Rd. Bilston UD	Kent Reeks	Male	24 Years	of Sydney. New South Wales Ships Engineer	Wilfully & maliciously murdered by some person or persons unknown	Certificate received from Allen Stokes Coroner for South West Staffordshire Inquest held Jan 22. 1914 & Feb 10. 1914	Eleventh February 1914	W. J. Colley Registrar.

CERTIFIED to be a true copy of an entry in the certified copy of a Register of Deaths in the District above mentioned.
Given at the GENERAL REGISTER OFFICE, LONDON, under the Seal of the said Office, the 20th day of July 19 84

DX 308554

This certificate is issued in pursuance of the Births and Deaths Registration Act 1953. Section 34 provides that any certified copy of an entry purporting to be sealed or stamped with the seal of the General Register Office shall be received as evidence of the birth or death to which it relates without any further or other proof of the entry, and no certified copy purporting to have been given in the said Office shall be of any force or effect unless it is sealed or stamped as aforesaid.

CAUTION:—It is an offence to falsify a certificate or to make or knowingly use a false certificate or a copy of a false certificate intending it to be accepted as genuine to the prejudice of any person, or to possess a certificate knowing it to be false without lawful authority.

GENERAL REGISTER OFFICE ENGLAND

Form A504M Dd 8264388 20M 6/83 Mcr(301479)

Notes on certificate of Kent Reeks

The address in Column 1 is an accurate one – Kent was killed outside – not in a house. On the other hand his home address is vague, probably because the accurate one was not known. The cause of death was typical of the time – it is not a cause at all really but a verdict! These days that column equivalent would give the cause of death, e.g. multiple injuries or perforation of the heart, and would give a verdict such as "accidental death" or "misadventure" or would have no further verdict if someone was to be tried for the death. There are two inquest dates three weeks apart. The first would have been opened to identify the body and take preliminary information and the second would have reached a conclusion about the death and its cause. Reproduced by kind permission of Mike Longworth.

else being aware of it, and the body may not be found for some time. In the case of an Inquest, the registration is not made until the Inquest has been held. In the last century that meant that there might be only a few days or up to two or three weeks between the death, the Inquest and the registration. These days, there can be many months between death and registration – or even over a year in a few rare cases.

The importance of the date of registration is that it dictates the appearance of the death in the indexes, as deaths are indexed by the date of registration and not the date of death. If you do not find a death registration in the quarter or even year that you expect it – look further on. It might have been that there was an Inquest.

If a death has not been registered within a year of the date of death, then the death cannot be registered except with the authority of the registrar general and this will be noted in the column with the date of registration.

Column 9 – Registrar's Signature

The last column is the signature of the registrar – and in the case of a death registered over a year late, the signature of the superintendent registrar as well.

Applying for your death certificate

The information about the headings and the use of the indexes is the same as for births and can be found on page 3. Similarly, the method of applying for your certificate is the same (see page 21).

NOTES

NOTES

NOTES

NOTES

NOTES

INDEX

INDEX